MW00514131

American Guys

By the same author:

CARS & Other Poems (o.o.p.)

Ladies, Start Your Engines: Women Writers on Cars & the Road (Faber & Faber, 1996)

Diamonds Are a Girl's Best Friend: Writers on Baseball (Faber & Faber, 1994)

American Guys

by

Elinor Nauen

Hanging Loose Press
Brooklyn, New York

Copyright © 1997 by Elinor Nauen

Published by Hanging Loose Press, 231 Wyckoff Street, Brooklyn, NY 11217. All rights reserved. No part of this book may be reproduced without the publisher's written permission, except for brief quotations in reviews.

Printed in the United States of America
10 9 8 7 6 5 4 3 2 1

Acknowledgments: Some of these poems have been published in the magazines *Baseball Diary, Exquisite Corpse, Hanging Loose, Humanities, KOFF, Long Shot, The Poetry Project Newsletter, RealPoetik, Scarlet, $lavery: Cyberzine of the Arts, Spitball, Talisman, Telephone, Tone, Transfer, The World* & possibly others; and in the anthologies *Diamonds Are A Girl's Best Friend: Women Writers on Baseball, Out of This World, The Stiffest of the Corpse, Innings & Quarters, Up Late: American Poetry Since 1970, American Poets Say Goodbye to the 20th Century,* and *Ladies Start Your Engines: Women Writers on Cars & the Road.*

Radiant gratitude to Maggie Dubris, Murat Nemet-Nejat & Johnny Stanton. A million thanks also to Edmund Berrigan, Blue Mountain Center, Andrei Codrescu, Ed Friedman, Nancy Graham, Bob Hershon, Janet Mullen, Alice Notley, Ben Strader, Chuck Wachtel, and other muses, readers, editors, critics & friends.

Cover art: *Natural History* by Louise Hamlin, from the collection of Ted Greenwald
Cover design by Caroline Drabik

Library of Congress Cataloging-in-Publication Data
Nauen, Elinor.
    American guys / Elinor Nauen.
      p. cm.
    ISBN 1-882413-41-5 (cloth). -- ISBN 1-882413-40-7 (paper)
    I. Title.
    PS3564.A8736A8   1997
    811'.54--dc21   96-40202
                        CIP

(continued on page 104)

CONTENTS

* *These started out being by Pablo Neruda. Without speaking (much) Spanish I "appropriated" his works & made these "versions" (not translations).*

For my father, Hans Nauen (1906-1986),
who would have been bemused & amused
to be considered either an American or a guy

Ha ha! My supernatural luck holds!
Even nature cannot assassinate me —
I am buffered by human desires!
—Jack Collom, *My Birds*!

PART I
American Guys

Old Habits Die Young

Here I am
opinions & all!

The History of Western Philosophy

Bertrand Russell had just about convinced me
there's more to life than sex
I'd like to go to bed
with him but he's dead   even windowless
monads are sexy   they remind me of gonads
careening around & bumping
each other   hitting on each other

I know more philosophy than that

you're not supposed to mix
your muse with your mistress or they'll both
fuck you   over   the real question
is
is there anything we can think of
which
by the mere fact that we can think of it
is shown to exist outside
our thought

the answer is sex
therefore god exists

sex is a revelation
a reason
empirical
possible   credible   self-consistent
the best of all possible worlds
sex precedes existence
precedes essence
I fuck   therefore
I attract every body with a force
directly proportional to the product

12

of their masses

Buridan's ass
unable to choose between 2 equidistant bundles of hay
died of hunger
call me up sometime   I'll make you lunch

Game 4, American League Championship Series, October 12, 1985

Bases loaded no outs & pitching on a mere 2 days rest
Dave Stieb looks so desperate I chew my fingers as tho
at a Stephen King movie, I can't watch alone!
so call Steve, who's sleeping
but amazingly enough Marion has the game on
not however imagining poor Dave
is as hounded as he looks to me

talk turns to tomorrow's reading
—oh man he just walked in a run—
I haven't really been watching you understand
typing all day
nothing like a reading to burrow for poems

Steve's a little depressed, Marion says,
he has to finish
all his poems
Yeah, I agree, I have about a million works
that're terrific till late innings then stop short

I'm getting a stomachache
watching Stieb claw around for help

And so is born another million-dollar scheme
The Relief Poet!
who'll come in at the end with a trick pitch
witty poignant heat
& finish off your poem   tidy up your poem
getting credit for a save of course

Then I remember for Marion
the incredibly short shortstop

the Royals used to have was Freddie Patek
& we 2 happy geniuses hang up
as Tom Henke comes in to get the inning's last out

The History of the Human Body
Winfield's Infield Hit
The Lassitude of the Infinite

Dear _____,
Hi, you can be in my new poem, if you're a Yankees fan.
Or, if you're a baseball fan (I just remembered
you're from the coast). Listen — as long as you're here
you might as well stay. It's just that I wanted
to write this poem about baseball
having 3 baseball titles & all
but one for you too, on the chance that's what
it'll take for you to be in love with me.
I used to seduce this gay friend that way —
a poem a day under his door —
the closest I got was the big IF:
if I ever, you'll be the one ....

My stomach leaping like a trout
& all I know is your eyes & mechanic's forearms.
Yeah, but what about this goddamn famous old-time
electricity: I haven't felt this way in years.
It's better than having a crush on
Lou Piniella & hooray
we're back to baseball.

José Cardenal once in winter ball
wouldn't play for 3 days cuz his uniform wasn't
     tight enough
oh the sex object
Winfield flings the ball to the shortstop
who wings it on in to the catcher
swinging Rick Cerone. It's the springtime
of philogeny & my ontogeny
is throbbing in all its bristly prehistoric cells.

16

I'm either having a nervous breakdown
or falling in love.
Yeah, so my favorite number is 14:
Lou's Yankee number of course
& my Nicaraguan lover,
a power hitter who smashed a homer the night after
& tipped his cap to me coming in to 3rd.
14 — my skirts plaid & too long, like my sentences
chalking Plato on the sidewalk, worrying
without grace, this in-between my baseball days.
At 10 I loved the Yankees cuz they won
at 25 love them again
for what I can't do — no self-consciousness
of body or mind, like perfect
conversation late at night, seamlessly caught.
I need my time of grace
hunt the beauties who will love me
ceaselessly.

I'm a terrible comedian because I have no
    sense of   timing
I gotta always say everything I think.
Flaubert said he'd rather die like a dog
than hurry by a second a sentence not ripe
I like those goddamn green bananas.

The Tucker Torpedo

Fierce as a bearcat I worry
You in the teeth of my love
Before I knew you I held out an arm
Saying dance little bearcat

Before you were born I loved you
In the back seat of an automobile
The party between my legs
I sat on your lap in a car named Blue

His forgotten face broods
In a swelter of promise
Unclaimed as prairie grass
Deep as last week

At times you can't help
But sentence 'em
Thoughts in the fire
Of the king of the road

My love cannot touch
Your lips titanic
Your concrete silence my love
Cannot touch love

If I were your teeth could I know
Your mouth better than my wild tongue
Before I knew you I held out an arm
Say goodbye little bearcat

I Smoke This Cigarette for You

take your shirt off let me see
your darkness my red bra your hands that see
what my words remember only while I sigh

when I wear my red bra
I always need to take off my shirt
but honey it's the same underwear

The August Furnace

I have put my mark on you
you need no tattoo
more rousing than
my kiss

the body & its fervor
are what concern
the august furnace
in hot embrace

lightning strafes
hotshot bicep
& on down
& down

The Jungle

a New Orleans jazz band
catches my desire
            in long blue notes

in tall green stalks
birds like corn
            and I shiver

XXXVIII (from 100 Love Sonnets)

I sleep in your house like an afternoon train
drowsy like doves, singing rococo

a rolling cascade made of thin rock
you laugh fleshily, palms flashing.
A blue light slides over outdoor stones
like whistling, waiting for a telegram

like Homer padding softly, fresh-voiced
birds fly into our boudoir.

I alone in the city have no voice
no end, no heart
to speak of the appearance of lions.

You, though, you sing, chant, you have plants—
flowers and lovers. You can write, eat,
return. You know you bring on winter.

Counting the Hats & Ducks

What I have in my pocket:
a pocket comb
a pocketknife
a pocket terror
a rocket scientist
a common loon
the loan of a commando, with many thanks
my hands
his hands
his undying etceteras
the best of dimes, the scent of dollars
the lounge chair that blew off the dock in last night's gale
the verdict
pesto & italian bread
sunlight soap, sun worship, son of man, sun fever,
someone else's passport
a small but well-chosen scientific library
the longing of a tender heart for word from her beloved

A Moustache and a Cigarette

Our favorite bar
where we head on post-aerobic Sunday afternoon
    and Johnny
explains Irish Sunday afternoons:
in bars.
We're not so different he says.
I like to think I'm not so different.
What were child Elinor's Sundays?

Johnny nudges: see that guy?

With one little dash of his eye at the bartender—
we've already cased her
beautiful high face, strangely lumpy body—I see
that guy's in love and she won't give him
the time of day: except of course she will
enough that he keeps mooning and drinking.

Knowing everything makes me feel smart
and drunk, my dad didn't have Sunday guys
I'm, like, first-generation guy
my eyes full of strange little dashes
anyone can see perfectly

Riding in Boats with Boys

for Nicholas

We go FAST, Ben cutting wheelies hard left,
and s-l-o-w
pittering up the channel.

Our roar churns two brown ducks from a cove
into a race.
Ben floors it.
They beat us anyway. I like how the birds leap
up & at 'em

in the moment

with the sun
in our hair
where the hills surge down to the shore

three white ducks dance in the light forever
free.

Going to a Game with You

is even more fun than going to L.A.
to see my words in her mouth
or following your prelude & hankering for an interlude
at a ballpark in Toronto New York San Francisco
or Boston where Cousin Bip's crazy mom
might take us to dinner & a miracle play
where the blue of your shirt would blond up your smile
so I liked looking at it and you
liked baseball in a smoke-ridden nightclub
in such a way that the windows roll down
& curves blow through my head
toolin' the prairie on a high summer night
singing this field forever.
Through concrete
to the green
of every ballpark we approach
from the dark to the day
we drive
somewhere
          it's always a game.

And we are not cheated of experience or hope
as we trace by starlight the roads where we played
    in the sun.

And we are not cheated of anything to come
for I can sing of it & you haunt the song.

Baseball Wife

She's thinking about him
He's thinking about scoring

Trojan

And then that summer my boyfriend gave me a car.
This was amazing as I was not that kind of girl
boys made grand gestures toward, my boyfriends
were the kind of morons who liked
smart girls.

Dave hung his arm over my shoulder—
his stiff Swedish version of a hug—& laid me up
against the last elm on the block that hadn't succumbed
    to disease.
"My Mustang," he said.
"Yeah," I said.
"I'm getting a Firebird," he said.
My other boyfriend Ken had a black Firebird.
We cruised up Main & down Dakota
for rubbery burgers at Teddy the Greek's drive-in
or to sneak in to the Dew Drop Inn.

"You can have the Mustang," Dave said.
"OK, cool," I said.
My parents would kill me so I figured he didn't mean it.

I called my friend Debbie whose dad let me park it
in their field where nothing but horseradish grew

till I thought to tell my folks
Dave was letting me drive it
that one last summer before we blasted off to college
or the army or the moronic jobs
my boyfriends would have for the rest of their lives.

Gas was 20¢ a gallon
a dollar's worth could gallop us halfway across the prairie,
a nighttime ride to wherever we weren't supposed to go.

Alas the hidden treacheries—the sparks, the shocks,
the struts & clutch I was heir to, what Dave wanted.

Chug a Lug: Poem for the Depression

The music was sexier than sex
Thinking about sex is sexier than sex
Mozart fucking me in the ear
Was sexier than whoever it was
Fucking me in the rear
       Ah the groupies! Ah the starfuckers!
I saw his red slashes
At the Modern & got someone or other
To introduce us & of course
He fucked me & as it turned out
The top of the tour was his etchings
       Well, well, I'm not cold but I keep
A blanket around me, I'm pretending
To be old, I'm pretending my face
Looks like I've lived my life, I still get carded,
By lovers who don't know whether they have to take me
Seriously, I have one foot
Out the door but some of me on the bed,
I wish I had an enormous belly so I could
Pretend to be a rock, I wish I
Pretend I forget I
Have one very pretty ankle the other
Got broken once the other got bit
By my dog once the other
Rubbed into subway gratings how can you call me cute
My eyebrows are too thick how can you call me cute
You just want to fuck me are you famous am I?
Winter's near you can keep me warm
Winter's here so are you so what
He'll fuck anyone but he has a crush on you
He'll fuck anyone
He'll fuck anyone
I may be easy but you'll fuck anyone

The Fatal Attraction

he's depressed he's shopping he's in great pain
I've destroyed his life with my fatal attraction conquest
femme fatale she who never
what he wants what is it he sees
I don't I shouldn't but I want I can't but
chatter on your book my book
a most unhilarious life
the one I meant to have & pushed too far & here we are
miserable & hard & nervous
I remember everything you ever said
I forget all the promises you think you made
& the anger I deserve
see the stigmata on my tongue?
I'm biting back retorts
patient as sea glass   huddled by the sea
I speak   translucent & smooth
he wants me   in some way   I don't   I turn
I'd rather live alone than with you
but I'd rather live with you than without you
but will you hate me till Wednesday please so I can
     get a little
more work done
he buys 4 bright tank tops & a pair of purple shorts
in the curtained dressing room we almost
I stagger against the wall when he slides his hand
under my shorts   dizzy
terror — would this never have happened?
he's trouble I'm trouble I know it I'm in trouble
let's go to your house
("our house" I say to myself)
& we do & make love then I don't
go with him to Sasha's play & he won't tell me he loves me
why not I scream but he's late & just says

you know
of course I don't   eat   I do
clip my red fingernails go to the movies say nothing
about anything to my friends who come visit & adore
me or don't
this week I'm into adoration
this week abasement to him & desire from everyone else
in 5 years I'll remember the passion the intensity
    the fatal
attraction & think   this was a good time
but right now I'm a jerk who fakes seizures
plus I want to step back behind the curtain
keep my life inside itself
its old routes   I get lost
going to work if I swerve the least bit

Wiener Roast

You, you wouldn't know love
if it bit you on the dick.

My punch has no force
for your tiny heart is scaled over
you bleating armadillo

The large and deliberate unterrored moments
are my cyclones—tatters to you

I was a fool
to think I could love a one
who has to be coaxed and coached
I was a fool to think
I'd want a piece of meat
someone else took a bite of already

Your emotions pay a dime on the dollar
you're an empty lot too stupid for weeds

Craven white-feather
flinch you must
from my telegraphic truth
fear ties you to the tracks
and you're flattened by the ghost of such as me

Risks are for fire-eaters
you, you drink milk and breathe through your nose
you eat raisins and live at home

Poor Guys
(Pobres Muchachos)

Who thinks on this planet
they can love tranquility?
Everyone sees and everyone interferes.

Ah, the terrible cost
when one man and one woman
after much soul-searching and attack
find they can't live apart.

I ask myself: if they watch carefully
and turn briskly, can't they twist
out of illegal sutures that disturb
their attentions—
I ask myself if the bull
hears the flapping of the matador's cloth
when he sees the cow.

Ah, the roads have eyes,
the parks — police.
There surely are hotels
... with windows that staple names;
deep canyons too murky and steep
for love; too much work ....

One man and one woman
at last obliged to flee
on a bicycle.

The Mornings Blossom into Noons

Sex used to be the way
to get a man to talk.

I traded sex to anyone
who could rock 'n' rant me into bed.

Too cute for words, beheaded by sex.

The blushing green is chased
around the autumn apple

By red confiding
& a warm afternoon.

I trust my mouth now not my youth.

American Guys

Jack, John, Ben
& I play pool
Polish bar   7th St   how
is it guys   all
know how to shoot
pool?   I sure don't.
hit 'em low
Ben says   I sink
three   in a row   never
done that before.
Johnny
walks in   I light
up   Jack, John and Ben
drink beer   Johnny ale
are we solid?
I ask   again   that goes
on your tombstone   John says.
I swill   Rolling
Rock   no one smokes
but the bar is smoky.
the bartender throws quarters
in the jukebox   I dance
alone.   Satisfaction.
I never had so many boyfriends
until I got married   they love me
for being happy
elsewhere.
Jack scratches.   I used
to know how to play
this game   he says.
Johnny hits 'em hard
        hmm—
he too   's done this before.

I let the guys
tell me what to do
next   for once
I'm the girl.
they line 'em
up.   I love
American guys.
saved from knowing
anything except   keep
one elbow up
skittering toward a side
pocket.

PART II
Landscapes

The Red Vine

When I hang out my wash I think of my baby
sleeping inside. She's five months now
& her earliest memory
hasn't happened yet. I wish mine hadn't I wish
I was my baby, sleeping
where the only color is poison
sumac & the sheets are cold & heavy
& what will become
of me. I'm a bad mother because that baby
is too much for me. She'll get away
but I never will.
The city so far
from earth & weather
& the sun watery & cold
& why does anyone live in the woods.
The postman
passes & sees me
so content
hanging out my wash.
Is there a place where women speak?

Backyards, Brooklyn

for Peggy DeCoursey

Spring tears
the slush
from magnolias & flowerpots & muscles.
Sunlight for Brooklyn.
Spring falsely
implies largesse
when in fact it's
work & scheming.
My neighbor will
soon draw off
the net
that protects his
bulbs. His neat clumps
will be full
of rocks. He'll shake
his head. Where'd they come from?
He can hardly believe
the earth as it spins
throws up such
reminders of the dead.

Maine

I have to get in
a car right
this minute and drive
a thousand miles. With
no purpose but
to sing   the corn
sings. It could be
1976 when I
lived in town eating
cream cheese
listening to Bruce
Springsteen hiding
on back streets
wishing my lover would
call on me. The hot
air was yellow: I
owned a car, held
out, drove
to the shore for clams. We
served enchiladas and feuds.
I drove home
3 a.m. because
of the children, glistening
Quebec French forties pop:
like songs
my mother
sang—happy
& betrayed.

Shall We Gather at the River

Shall we gather at the river
Where angel feet have trod?
At the bottom of the river
Your hair dragged by weeds.
Are you waiting for a savior
As the bottom of the river
Scrapes your clumsy bones.
Shall we gather at the river
And curse our tangled love?
For when the Savior's spoken
Our ears are filled with mud
And we'll gather by the river
To be washed out to sea.

Storm Surpassing

Golden fields hum.
The red barn throws off a thousand summer days
in barns, never knowing
what would be under that straw. Kisses.
Remember how it felt to surrender
to pinching rain, the whipping of wind?

And hugging when you're wet inside
your skin. The empty farmhouse
its wooden floors, overhead bulbs
black & white photos of dead uncles' weddings.
No porch, no lawn, a field
in shadow, all but some sun
flung like a sleeping arm.

And I feel lonely. Was I the girl
who stood caught in silence in a summer storm?
Was there once a girl in this pivot of the world?

July Hay

On the prairie the wind is constant as the sky.
Men in jeans, straw hats & long-sleeve shirts
bend into their scythes, resigned to an afternoon
    in the sun.
They find depth in the thickness of the soil.

The land switches like a cat's tail
between hay and clover.
High-summer trees are deep as caves.

A man lies on woman-curved earth
a straw in his mouth, thick slabs of sandwich at hand
a lifetime of yellow hay, fat flowers & wind.

A Sparrow on the Riviera

Why don't those flirts —
she with parasol & white embroidered dress
he with top hat, pale shirt & ivory-headed cane —
why don't they pause elsewhere
or turn out to sea
where a dozen boats pitch toward their promenade.
And Mamà, sitting on a Sunday
in a stiff cane chair,
why doesn't Mamà snooze a little, or stroll
to the edge & stare at her youth out to sea.
Leave the vines & mass
of red & milky flowers
to one who cares not for clouds
a last clean fall day
or fair forever
just now found by those flirts.

Summer Ride

A local in wide-brimmed white hat
watches me dig for a dollar
on afternoon-empty ferry.
He picks up a newspaper abandoned
on a bench. I look across him
at the blue water of the sound
pure green trees beyond.
The ferry's high ceiling is yellow as August.
Silence swallows even the flap of the engine.

I rode my bike by the river

& the heat crawled around me
through thick leaves
onto the sidewalk
& I stood
on sidewalks of the past
driven by the heat
into bliss.
Goodbye to August's perfect heat. Goodbye!
& white shoes
& the wind
in full trees.

From Williamsburg Bridge

A girl in white
in the window.
Radio
plays softly
a Joplin rag.
Soon she'll creak
across the room
fix supper
for her cranky father.
She is in the whole building
the only one
home. Children
play stickball.
Men and women buy
shoes
and fruit.
America is rich
& always possible.

Glad All Over

I should look at flowers more, yes.
I would ID that thick stem & red spray
zigzag leaf
& the difference between furled rose & tulip.
I could sit in the garden, wonder
about the miracle of life.
My friend M—— knows the meaning of life.
Who doesn't? It's to be in our lives
& we really have no choice
so that's settled. It's just that some
people are happiest when they're miserable.
Some people made one giant mistake
& keep paying long after they learned
everything they needed. Happy every minute
that's me. Blossoming. Gigantic.

The Conventional Arm of
Commercialized Country Music

When I was 16 I lived for the summer with my father's Uncle Jerry, an old man with pale hair & a wen on his nose. He lived on the edge of a small lake, where he made his living trawling for drowning sailors, of whom there were few. He believed he would be successful by setting up shop where there was little competition. Using the wealth he'd inherited from his grandfather, a composer of popular ballads, he had, variously, launched a botanica on Beacon Hill, an ice emporium at the North Pole, & a mountaineering supply outlet at the entrance to the vast plains of Outer Mongolia. Uncle Jerry introduced me to a fellow who used the line "Want to give me a back rub?" as a way to pick up girls. Did it work? he was asked. "The first time," he said, "but never again." Someone pointed out that the custom is to offer a back rub not ask for one. I believe a plan that works brilliantly the first time it's attempted should be forsaken forever. And then the pickup threw a rod & spoiled the engine.

Three More Things

There is a tiny car on a tiny bureau by a tiny pink comb. The man with small ears kisses a tall woman with long brown hair. He smoothes his right hand between her shoulder blades and on down to the little hollow above where her buttocks flare—the "small." With his left hand he folds her hair around her neck, then kisses her lips. Her hair is so long it wraps around her neck twice. He pulls hard, yanks till it completes a third revolution. Her pale peachy skin darkens into apricot. Her tongue flops out of her mouth & the kiss becomes limp on her part, ever more passionate on his. She flails her right hand toward the bureau, reaching for the rattail comb. She hopes to puncture his heart & thus be freed. Instead her hand lands on the tiny car. He gets in & hits the road.

Any man who stares like a prophet

"It is a scream
it is a night
it is like a child
it is a tiger behind bars"

rings a living sound, like the roar from the lion's breast

Blue Moon

The bar had pool tables, pinball, a dartboard.
In the blinking shine of a Coors sign
I shoved dimes in the jukebox.
"Tonight the Bottle Let Me Down"

I got on the phone
cupping an ear
against the waa-waa hiccups—
"A Little Bit of Soul"

then stepped out
                    leaned
into the dark pan of desert sky.
White bits that once were stars waved.

    Where was I
    dreaming across this sky that strained
    against me and my dying father.
    "Darkness, Darkness"

I tried sentences, aloud to that foreign sky:
    "I am 34 years old and my father is dying."
    "My entire life I have been a daughter, a person
      with a father."
    "I am in Arizona and my father might have died."
"Blue Moon of Kentucky..."
Patsy Cline's weeping
"...keep on shining, shine on the one that's gone
    and left me..."
Patsy's voice clear as the desert air
"...blue. It was oh on a moonlit night, stars..."
laced out
"...shining bright, Whispered on high, your love said..."

of a roadside bar on the edge of Phoenix
"...goodbye."

I drove on while Patsy
still aimed her song
thin as an arrow
                    at the moon

& one shining star collapsed somewhere in the sky.

The Cold Dark Sea

for Augusto Lori

I lie with my hands
between my legs, I know to run
hot water—when we get hot water—
in the sink to give my toes a lick
before I dash into bed
with all my socks on, the holes of one
underlapping the bare threads of another.

Tomorrow I'll find a newspaper & stuff it in the holes.
Why build a house with slats. Why open it
to the cold wind that floods my room.
I push against it till it punches me, if I could lie pliant
the wind would be a friend.
But it's too cold for thoughts to think me warm.

The wind has bit off bits of the curtain
& who would want to see me lying in the kind of sleep
cold allows, you barely breathe
you save everything for dreaming but dreams skip
around your naked neck so
you dream of penguins, polar bears, outdoor straggle
snowblindness
small boats cast adrift.
Swimming in the cold dark sea.

Winter, Monhegan Island

The light falls yellow & cold
on a lobsterman's shack,
who is himself in deep
shadow in a dinghy under a fjord
on Maine's rock-
dammed coast.
Pink in the water
a trick of the afternoon
light that gives Maine austerity
and strange
seaflowers that bloom
off the snow
where the cold is blue
& gold & the sun steel
on salt water
for the snow devil's attack.
Air beats into his lungs.
The barn abides.

The Green Car

God what a morning!
The snow so beautiful when it settled on the Square
but that was last night, when we kicked & kissed
& the moon clawed its way through lavender snow clouds
& we laughed & kissed. And now the snow & you
have the morning grumps, so I went out
to find you the perfect present & the sun
was so bright I couldn't keep my eyes open
so I snubbed your mother, quite by mistake
& oh dear I'll hear about it for weeks
& my feet are cold & wet & if the streetcar splashes I'll
toss my head at the driver.

My squinting puts wrens in the fountain.
My snappy breath springs up lilacs.
The driver is smiling.
It's not such a bad morning after all.
We'll walk again tonight
& the streets will be dry.
The snow hugging us with white.
The moon thrown aside.

PART III
Now That I Know
Where I'm Going

Tell the County Librarian to Shut Up

My forthcoming work
in 5 volumes
The Neglect of Cheese in European Literature
is a work of such unprecedented & raucous
detail that it is doubtful
I shall live
to finish

On the Bus

As much sky tonight in NYC as buildings
along First Ave
on the bus
I'm overcome
Becky's birthday and I am on my way
8 white wagons and 3 radios
summer at work and some
are going to work
A surveyor strolls the UN grounds, expansive and proud
everyone is beautiful
and relieved, it's only a dollar
only a dollar and we can ride
into the night that bears your name
There's Queens down 34th St, wide open
the Nebraska of New York
I'm not a 14th-century serf and I am no tycoon
white dress, bare legs, 93°
Comfort me, come to me
"I love you my heart is innocent"
Where are you going
July New York?

Life on the Prairie

Dawn explodes 'cross Dakota field
as though it's never been before
with me the watcher
of skies that couldn't be this scarlet
    hearkener
    to a train whistle
    blown through my heart, cheaply,
    like a TV show I thought was memory.
Everything's where it should be
but no one's where they could be.
    Hank Williams had no choice
    'cause he split a song with the jagged roar
        of lightning.
    Who would have known if he'd up and quit?
    Just another young man dead.
Lulled by the lowing cows
he cried with the wolf
seizing lonesome prairie howls
    to a song that scares
    a hitchhiker full of stories
    who resents such joy
and when they drop me off
I stare at the black soil darker and darker
from whence comes corn
flakes and fritters and gritty ears
full of the germ. It all starts and ends.
Everything's what it could be
but no one's where they should be.
    A kid kicks out a thumb and finds a brother
    or the song that never came again.
It's colder and more sorrowful
in the bay of morning
when you're happy by the road

waiting for a song
 as the sun comes
 into your life again and again.

On the Road with William Carlos Williams

Leaving for Maine in the morning
I can't decide
between *Pictures from Breughel* and *Paterson.*
Oh me oh my.

I almost always take Breughel.
I used to take Paterson.

Once two truck drivers picked me up hitching.
It was too noisy for the usual where-ya-froms
& I pulled out Paterson
which one said he'd read in school.

They took me on a tour of a steel mill in Gary
Indiana in the dawn.

Spring Training

for Becky

Full speed ahead! in fact it
is here & alas I am there that is to say
I am here & the Yankees are in Florida
where the green & blue are extreme & particular
and a blaze of sun anoints the heroes
of a ruthless nostalgic crowd
of dreamers. Dave Winfield is wearing
wire-rim glasses & describing his education.
I am in right field with a catcher's mitt
playing for the Twins in pinstripes &
self-consciousness. The newspapers make very little
of a woman making the team. Nor do they think it strange
I'm as old as Dave. Dave does though.
Your unlined skin! he marvels. Your jet-black hair!
And an autodidact to boot.
Boot an easy fly, I mutter nervously.
Dave looks stern. What do you call an Irishman
who's been buried for 50 years?
Billy Martin? I suggest.
Pete! He laughs, I laugh, we all laugh.
It is spring & it is baseball & the Yankees
are guaranteed a world championship
& life is as simple as a slow roll foul
down the first base line.

Ballad
(Balada)

Come on — a guitar sang — to me
of forests coloring, waving on cold plains
under a sky curved with anguish

A drunk enters a tavern weaving under wine
a hat pulled down over his eyes
he stumbles in his shoes
pisses on his feet, blesses everyone
with yellow hands

I never returned through those gates
but instead sleep through the hours —

dishonored and clouded

while the heart forces a smile.
When they say that to be ethereal
is to forget facts —
                    then I'll take a guitar
passing a little time till time exists no more.

With my hat full of grapes
I'll ask for that old guitar —

nothing goes, nothing comes —

the door no longer resists —

The Fire
(El Fuego)

.

In the musical moment
a river spoke to me
shunting its waters together and to me:
It scoots over rocks
singing, following highways
while I watch with eyes
more furious than its turbulence.

We are dedicated
to the vanishing thought
as the evening earth.
I love the solitude
and already count on nothing.
I don't go to sky or earth.

We exaggerate
saying we'll return to the fog
but instead hike in bright days
with laurel boughs
stumble on red llamas
with a stern eye toward town.
I soon open the papers,
prisoner of the revolving toward cities.

Enigma with a Flower
(Enigma con una Flor)

Victory. It's late, not absolute.
I take, as spoils, to my love
a white worker who disturbed
the eternal immobility of earth,

clearly formed by the devil
but from the sun, a white ray, a spilled dash of milk.

Dead Man's Daughter

We dance in the thin light of his skin
This world shall no more be a home
We dance down the drift of memory
A pearl is no purified bone

Touring in the Car of Dreams

We are driving on the island
The splendid glories
Of a vivisectionist past
Are scattered on the island

A sense of direction:
        No more than the wind
        Or the earth as it spins

        As dust mesmerized by a lightbulb
The driver is drawn to a jag

        A subtle red car after dusk
Blinks as it drives into doom

Yuan Chi died of grief
On hearing of the execution
Of his friend Chi Kang

Neither car nor its shadow
        (Certain days, certain keys)
A shadow is only a shadow
No more than speed
Or the car as it dims

                Driving
                    & Singing:
                That tree
                That tree
                That tree
                That telephone pole

Your Lucky Day

You who once sat in the cafés of Neptune
taking flight on invisible ink
pale unto vanishment: listen and tilt.

             People here know how to die, he said,
          his legs hitched up on a chair

Out East? I said
No way numbskull, I said
you don't know Dakota roads—
straight no potholes flat no cops.
I drive a pale car.

          He got new teeth and now has AIDS
          Grave beyond fear   grave beyond the field
          O Western road! Sling me high above
the rising sun
light sun bright first sun
I see
wish I may wish I might
This wish

What is all that up ahead?
Rewind
The Hopis had it right
The past is what you see
Rewind
And the future is behind
The unborn and the dead
Sleep comes to all.

                    Faster
            Faster than your breath can leave you
The radio breathless as noise
            The dark renunciation of night on the prairie.
The empty road foreshadows
a million empty galaxies.

The dark is come upon the sun
dying thus around us every day.

            A baby comes into this world
            and is given a rattle.
            80 years later he goes out
            that rattle in his throat.

Say there's a hundred people whose deaths
would diminish you. Say you're 30 or 35
with 50 years left.
That's two funerals a year
till the end of time.

This empty road the start
 a hundred empty worlds.
   The dark is come upon the light
     dying thus around us every day.

      He wears a cloak of human bones
      beating steel drums with dynamite sticks.

            Only the ford lets him cross
            though circling takes me back again.

      All I really want is for no one to die
      for the world to run transfixed so I can love my darlings
      with all my might.

Driving driving   till I finally come down

The Expanding Universe

Driving along the prairie
Until first light
Not knowing till first dawn
If it's winter or fall:
Car steamy   feet warm.
Subtle tender crawl of bright
Into the dusty windscreen
And I shake the nighttime deejay, nighttime
Long sweeping push
To get there, get going and get there:
There's room
For expanse. Little purple field-flowers
Luminescent in my frayed vision.
I stop at the first town and give away some old shirts.
Gas spurts like love. Like coffee
The smell of gas soars.
The driving
As though grass ripens any old time.

Task Force

He's an Eisenhower Republican and he knows what
that means
    But you don't
He can use the subjunctive correctly in a sentence
    But you can't
He washes his socks at night in the kitchen sink
    But you slob
He's a boat people helper he says shoot 'em all
    And bushwhack
He's 14 1/2 times more likely to get assassinated
    Than you are
He banned the Charleston from the Soviet Union
    Machine Dance
He clogged the Sierra Mujeres till they bawl occupied
    So polite
He knows the names of all the countries in Africa
While you dress like Ralph Nader to play in a band
    On Death Row
He's floated past more than the Staten Island
  Ferry Terminal
    So go home!

Right Thinking

We discard our white men's names!
From this day forth we will be known as

Elinor Oldsmobile	Blind Lemonjello
Maggie Crockpot	Bonnie AquaFresh
Rachel Timex	Olga L. L. Bean
Tim Tampax	Johnny Q. Public
Granpa Palmolive	Edie Minnesota Twins
Ann Marlboro	Danny Pet Rock
Alice Howard Johnson	Jeff Boy-Ar-Dee
Bob The Bronx	Eddie Money
Jim UMass	Jane Curtain
Elizabeth New Jersey	Hank Snow
Edselm Tubb	Ford Madox Ford

Time Is

Time as long
as a barn is wide
fast as mosquitoes

And us just a speckled studebaker
headed for the big crash.
Time goes
like a murder along the road.
When will you stuff it in your pants?

Found Poem

(from Phil Rizzuto)

Why would they have
seedless watermelon in a seed
catalogue?
They're trying
to make watermelon
extinct.
I call it
genocide.

Now That I Know Where I'm Going

I'll never be a junkie cuz I can't stand menthol cigarettes
    A novelist since I sleep like a fat pink pig
I'll never be a speed freak cuz I hide the bottle & forget
    where it is
        A great lover cuz I make jokes in bed

When I dress for success they send me to the moon
    till I remember there's a game on &
I'll never be a big homerun hitter for the Sox (why not?
why not?)
    cuz I throw like a girl & I can't hit the ball

If I go get the operation that gives you great cheekbones
    I'll still have to get the one that puts my eyes
        farther apart
& I'll still never be a great actress
    cuz I only know how to faint & disrobe

I'll never live in Paris because the French live there
    I'll never have a baby cuz they'd never let me
        name her Fort
I can't be a milkman cuz people would make rude jokes
    or a garbageman because I couldn't stand
        to throw all that perfectly good stuff away
I'll never be Queen for a Day cuz they took it off the air

So suck my dick & I don't even have one

If I Ever Grow Old:
Grim and Gleeful Resolutions

for Janet
after Swift

To be grumpy, grouchy, petulant, paranoid & mean: to
  hit out with my cane
     from my wheelchair at passersby
To clutch my chest, hold my breath, turn blue & be
  allowed everything
To insist upon senior citizen discount
To constantly remind the whippersnappers that if it
  was good enough in my day
     it's too good for them
To remind the Young that I knew them when younger;
  to poopoo their feats
To make children kiss me on my scrofulous cheek & if
  it makes them cry
     because I smell funny, to slap them
To make them push me fast in my wheelchair but if
  they tip me
     they should've known better
To scare the wits out of the Young: It goes so fast, one
  day you're young,
     the next you're like me, old & slow, how did I
       ever get to be so old . . .
     it'll happen to you. To never let them forget this
To give up shopping & dressing, as no one wants to
  fuck me so why bother
To help, with the accumulated wisdom & authority of
  my years, all those who suffer:
To cut off mercilessly anyone who interrupts
To become extremely set in my ways, obsessive,
  hypochondriacal, opinionated, argumentative,
  obstinate & indomitable

To remind One & All of my various former loves &
    enumerate those once infatuated   with me:
To be grumpy, grouchy, petulant, paranoid & mean:
    to hit out with my cane from my wheelchair
    at passersby
To insist upon senior citizen discount
To become extremely set in my ways, obsessive,
    hypochondriacal, opinionated, argumentative,
    obstinate, indomitable & forgetful

PART IV

How Hans Became
an American

Blindman's Holiday

Twilight—the hour between when one can no longer
    see to read
and the lighting of the candle—is called blindman's
    holiday.
In blindman's holiday, no work is done.

Out of the belly of hell cried I . . . And the Lord spake
    unto the beast
and it vomited my family out upon the dry land.

No-Passing Pesach: Someone I didn't know very well
invited me to her family's for Passover. When the meal
was served, they loaded the table with platters of food.
Except then it all just sat there. Nobody handed anything
around. I ate only what was in arm's reach—no turkey,
no salad, only beans and pearled onions and seltzer.

I believe in the sun even when it's not shining.
I believe in food even when I'm not eating.
I believe in God even when He devours his children.

Eve serving only a worm-ridden apple from her
    bounteous garden.

Mother's Day Plague: I sent my mother a Hallmark card:
"You've been like a mother to me."

When spring comes, the earth peels away and the dead
    find themselves
whiter than before.

Summer, when bones bake open.

July 4th fret: Where was anyone who could carry a tune at our Independence Day Hootenanny?

I smell autumn coming like a hound.

Fiasco of San Gennaro: Under the cover of merriment, a man was shot with a small gun at a street festival in Little Italy. He was fat and in his fall knocked heavily into a sausage-and-peppers cart. Grease flew everywhere, scalding a baby, my sister. My mother and father had no health insurance, and my sister was scarred for life. Embittered, she ate her way through Italian festivals, becoming fat as a house, until one time a man offered her $10 million dollars if she would either (a) sleep with Barry Manilow (b) drink a glass of urine or (c) eat a regurgitated hot dog. She ate the regurgitated hot dog, became wealthy beyond her wildest dreams and never spoke to any of us again.

Christmas Conflagrations: Once, my aunt's neighbor went to church on Christmas and set the oven on clean instead of cook, reducing a 20-pound turkey to ash. When the guests arrived, they ate pie . . . Advised by his girlfriend not to bring anything the first time he went home with her for the holidays, my brother took no gifts; everyone in her large family gave him something . . . . While my married friends shot heroin and threw up in the bedroom, I sang carols with their two sets of parents . . . . A form of hemophilia is called Christmas Disease.

Hanukkah Carnage: My father died on the second night of Hanukkah, many years ago. Deep calls to deep, out of the belly of hell cry I.

New Year's Eve Breakdown: I was evicted from my first New York apartment on the last day of the month, which happened to be December. The only place I knew of was from an ad in the *Village Voice* for "student and transient rooms" on West 39th Street, which I didn't know was near Times Square. When I walked up the long front hall, a note taped to the Plexiglas read: Short Stays (Up To 1 Hour), $4; 1 To 4 Hours, $6; Up To 24 Hours, $10.

New Year's Downfall: My mother blew all the fuses an hour before a New Year's Eve party. Guests entered a house smoothly lit with candles, and a Bohemian trend in parties began in Sioux Falls, South Dakota. Many people found fucking among the furs irresistible. My sister was conceived in that ill-lit bedroom where the coats were thrown.

Twilight . . . the hour when we can no longer see to rejoice.
Hearts along the calendar, winter to winter,
seem enchanted, stones that devour the living.

If we can just get through December
the rest of the year won't be so bad.

The Soprano

Bored with her own brilliance
She worries
If she really cuts loose
Her hat will fall off
Her midnight pile of a hat

Pink boa and jungle leaf
Her mascara'd eye
Arrogant arrow of an eyebrow
In red profile her red mouth
Scribbles an echo down arm and looming bosom.

Glittering beauty plucked up courage.

The soprano's hat flew off.

Red she grew, and very warm.

Breakfast, 1914

They get the coffee they expect
and sit knees touching
under the best piece of furniture they own,
a grained table with heavy, worked legs;
the New World wrestles with the Old.
She is worked up about a package and a newspaper.
He waits for her to pass him the sports section.
The last half cup is for him. He thinks about changing
his name and she imagines herself taller.
They painted the floor and walls the same deep blue
and now wonder if they should paint them lily-white
or a hue made of only proximity.
She kisses him and turns her face to the lusterless dawn.

The Cat's Dream
(Sueño de Gatos)

The beautiful cat sleeps with weight and limbs

but such cruel bones, true blood
with all the rings of everything

that circle
the geology of earth

and firmament
the color of earth

I want to sleep like a cat
with all of time's balls

with night's tongue
sex afire

till nothing more need be said
more tender than Atlas under the world

directing it crazily

Caesar of dreams

He undulates, this sleeping cat: drinks the night
like dark water, despairing, careening through

his dreams or mine, nakedly panting,
sleeping mighty as a tiger, as light as salt.

Sleep ... sleep, cat of my night
with your ceremonial priests lying on stone:
order our dreams, stretch and shine them

with lilting things and long sweep of your tail.

Dead Portraits
(Retratos Muertos)

It's so much work to remain immortal!
and until now I've barely succeeded
(I whisper in my stupors and my sleep)

Anytime we humans move
it's a detour so we can maintain
our shadow, yes señor, in these battles.

(And those gifts — the same old ones
of peace and death, wash through and chill our memories
erasing all others without end: pictures of our fathers
bigoted and sharp till they're dead like ourselves.)

This infernal restlessness, killing unto death,
and now we think we've achieved immobility
— but those stealing out of the street
have taken with them our portraits.

Monte Alban

In the green
Solitude

A man
Throws a ball
Through a stone
Hoop   ripples
Down narrow
Stairs
Stones
Like water   falling
From time
Into mystery

Earthbound, a man
Leaps beyond

The world

Has always been
A world
Of exiles

No Safety

All that hate me whisper together against me,
against me do they plot my death.
Yea, my old familiar friend,
in whom I trusted,
who did eat my bread,
has lifted up his heel against mine.
—Psalm 41

I

I pick my friends according to whether they
    would hide me.
Once you're betrayed it's too late to choose better.

Jews like to argue
who was worst:
The French? in 1940, five million
wrote poison-pen letters
denouncing individual Jews.

No, the Austrians—Hitler, Eichmann, Waldheim.
All Austrians.

No, no, the Rumanians
who outraged even the Germans
when they failed to bury the bodies of those they
    murdered.

The war lost, some Nazis jumped into stripes and
    yellow star—
the Russians shot them all the same.

Some Jews survived death camps and went home

and the Poles shot them
their neighbors, the Poles
their neighbors shot them.

Why bother to shoot the dead?

II

After Theresienstadt is it obscene to sing?
Unseemly to be alive
when such effort was made to stomp their bones?

"They"?
Say "we"
we Jews   still here.
My dear little father ran
rather than give over his bad (gold-filled) teeth.

The Jews are historians—remember,
in every generation some rose
against us but we were saved. Who
saved us? Who saves me?
What happens to one
happens to all. If my aunt is killed, where are her bones?

> Hopeful and over-obedient,
> they and we, the scared and the slow,
> neglected political and military science and so were
> twice-naked.

The voice of history
divides the flame of fire.
We don't conquer we merely persevere.
How long will—   will the world look on?
Gnashing upon me with my teeth.
My babies, my children

it's so hard to raise
the dead.

III

I am a Jew.

I announce this
so I won't hear what I do hear when people don't guess
so I can't be a coward, so I can't deny anything.
No way out.
When I stay silent, my bones
wax old through my roaring
all the day long.

 . . . But my mother is English
doesn't that make me
half WASP shouldn't I be more
tactful? No one
wants to hear it why don't I
shut up? No one wants to hear it
and why should they
I wasn't there
they weren't there they
didn't do it.

The voice of history divides my flame from the fire.

The necromancers arouse themselves with the bones
    of the dead.
They warm the bones with their bodies
they insert the bones into their nostrils
they incite the bones to answer their questions
I shout at the bones until I am hoarse.

"It would have done no good to protest
they would only have turned on
us
this way at least we got
a case of good wine out of it
a country house
when the old owners
suddenly
decided to leave the country."

The Jews have only their history.
We must remember—but why should we live
for the dead?
The irony of history divides the flames of fire.
I am cursed with memory. My life is spent with grief
and my years with sighing.
My bones are consumed.

No safety.
That's all I'm trying to say.
Next time take me first,
I already know as much as I need to.

IV

Why should I have
resentments? Didn't
my friend's husband say
he couldn't believe
I am a Jew
and didn't he mean
he likes me and he doesn't like
Jews
and aren't I flattered
to be told I'm not like
them

aren't I flattered to be
my own person not
the product of a people half as old as time?

One must forgive one's enemies
but not before they have been hanged.
                        —Freud, quoting Heine

V

My friends think it strange
I carry three passports.
My money's in jewels, my bags are packed.
I pick the friends I pray
will hide me.
Once you're betrayed
it's too late. I am cursed

with memory
the flames divide me from my past.

I am indebted to Susan Neiman & her book
Slow Fire: Jewish Notes from Berlin
for material in this work.

To Hans in Heaven

where you're playing cards
peeking over the tops of your glasses
into the angels' hands.
And they wonder
if they saw it wrong
but know you added right
smooth finesse that works
to your serene trump.
Your noisy American kid
wants to phone you in heaven
hear you say how are you, little one,
but it's enough to think you're doing
the tax returns of the stars
slouching on your cloud patio
turning off the moon to save on the electric bill
playing patience, dealing solitaire,
bridge from one world to another.

How Hans Became an American

I've been sitting at my desk a lot
staring at my father.
It's a picture taken in summer
a few months before he died.
He's looking at me
with a wry and knowing
—did he know?—
expression. He looks like a man
who needs a private joke
to get a proper snapshot.
He's looking straight at me, even as I sit
in a cold May, a little too tired,
the Yanks getting beat 4-1 in the 5th
by Oakland out on the coast,
a lackluster they'll-never-catch-up game
Rasmussen not getting shellacked
just doesn't have anything
and neither do the hitters.
Gone native in his Arizona retirement
Dad is wearing a bola tie and looks shrunken, frail.
I liked to kiss him on the top of his bony head
in the desert mornings.

He took all of us to a game only once, my first, I was ten,
Charlie was eight, Lindsay was twelve
and the baby was left home.
We drove all the way from South Dakota
up to Minneapolis
to see the Twins play the Yankees (my team).

Daddy was a refugee from Nazi Germany
and Mom was English.
They were grown-ups
who'd never seen a game either. They went
because he was the father of Americans
and I was a little baseball fanatic.

Mom sat quietly for about twenty minutes
fanning herself with a straw sunhat and beaming
then asked, when does the game begin?
Look down there, we said.
It was already the second inning but I still don't think
she spotted it.
I think she was waiting for the play by play.
The familiar radio sounds
so different in the ballpark.

Daddy wore plaid shorts over his white skinny legs
and puffed a cigar.
He began to like baseball
when he found someone
who knew less about it than he did.
He explained it all to Mom
mostly according to his own logic.
He had an accountant's sense of symmetry
and the diamond pleased him.
The profusion of numbers and their richness
impressed him,
the implication of infinity.
And it was a damn nice summer day.
I think now of those bleachers
old Metropolitan stadium full of stolid Scandinavians
who never corrected him—
that would have spoiled their fun.
Mom would ask, Where's that chap running off to now?

And Dad would explain:
He goes home because he has nowhere else to go.

My brother and I spent most of the game under the stands
scrapping with baby Twinkies—
Twins fans who didn't take to our rooting for the
enemy.
Charlie thinks he remembers a game-winning
Bobby Richardson grand slam.
I only recall the Yanks winning in the 10th
and the incredibly intense luxury of that lagniappe inning.

Daddy stuck with baseball too.
Like the voting that made him proudest as a naturalized
    citizen
he quietly exulted
in being able to talk to his kids
about what they liked to talk about
which was sports. What pleasure
it gave him
to be able to call
    (those Sunday calls!—this is later
      after we'd all left home)
and say, "So, Mattingly's still leading the league" or
"I see where the Yankees aren't doing too well."
But tonight there's an amazing comeback
another 10th-inning heroic to call home about
    ("I see where the Yankees are going great guns")
though it's a few second basemen later
and the serene and splendid Willie Randolph
who pulls it out for the team.

Hanging Loose Press thanks the Fund for Poetry and the Literature Programs of the National Endowment for the Arts and the New York State Council on the Arts for grants in support of the publication of this book.

 Produced at The Print Center, Inc., 225 Varick St., New York, NY 10014, a non-profit facility for literary and arts-related publications. (212) 206-8465